University of Minnesota
FREDERICK R. WEISMAN
ART MUSEUM, MINNEAPOLIS

DISTRIBUTED BY THE
UNIVERSITY OF MINNESOTA PRESS

WEISMAN ART MUSEUM    FRANK GEHRY DESIGNS

# THE BUILDING

# THE WEISMAN ART MUSEUM

## THE BUILDING

When the Weisman Art Museum opened on November 22, 1993, Herbert Muschamp of the *New York Times* declared, "A new, stainless-steel art museum has five of the most gorgeous galleries on earth." Nearly sixty years after the museum's humble beginnings as the Little Gallery in the upper floors of a Beaux Arts-style auditorium on the University of Minnesota campus, it moved into its first permanent home – and what a home! Frank Gehry designed a house that we could make a home for our collections, programs, and people. With our rebirth in a shiny "ice castle that doesn't melt," we became the Frederick R. Weisman Art Museum, honoring a native Minnesotan who, like Frank Gehry, made good in his adopted city of Los Angeles. Ten years later, the Weisman remains the most adventuresome architecture in Minnesota – and proves that a building can be a design landmark and exceptionally functional at the same time.

The museum is located in the center of the Minneapolis campus atop what was once a parking lot on a hill overlooking the Mississippi River and downtown Minneapolis. The Weisman appears to be a lighthouse or a beacon sitting high above the river. Its faceted stainless-steel west façade can be viewed as a continuation of the craggy river bluffs.

The giant sculpture that is its west side changes constantly with the weather and time of day. Stainless-steel panels, or "fish scales" in the language of Frank Gehry's work, break up and reflect light, giving the building energy and movement. On a bright day the building is iridescent, sparkling in the sunlight like the river below. At sunset, the west side is on fire, blazing with the reflection of the setting sun. At night it becomes a twinkling star, catching headlights of passing cars and the colored lights of downtown.

The east and south sides of the building, facing the student union and a dormitory, are clad in an orangey brick. Behind these walls are the museum's exhibition galleries — spaces that require long, unbroken walls for hanging paintings. These walls pay homage to the essential character of the University of Minnesota campus: brick. Most buildings on the Minneapolis campus mark their brick-ness with mixed colors or mortar that separates and empha- sizes each block. The bricks of the Weisman walls are all one color and the mortar is carefully dyed to match. The walls strike the eye as flat planes — foils for the energy of the stainless-steel sculpture of the west side. The expected is reversed: the steel emphasizes individual units and the bricks appear a single sheet.

Most university students enter the museum on the north side, through the main entrance intended for pedestrians. Students inevitably flow toward the museum as they exit the covered walkway above the Washington Avenue Bridge over the Mississippi. As they approach the museum from the opposite direction, coming from Coffman Memorial Union toward the bridge, a sail-shaped canopy over the museum's main entrance frames the skyline of downtown Minneapolis, beckoning students to come in. Two large windows pierce the north wall of the exhibition galleries to allow passersby a glimpse of the art inside. A "sun scoop" shades these windows in summer and reflects light onto the bridge in winter. During construction, workers dubbed the canopy and the sun scoop "the potato chip" and "the Frito."

The bold, evocative forms of Frank Gehry's designs elicit strong opinions. When the museum opened, a local wag likened the stainless-steel exterior to an exploding silver artichoke. Some people are reminded of works of twentieth-century art, such as cubist sculpture by Pablo Picasso or the Dadaist creations of Marcel Duchamp. Others have compared it to an impressionist painting by Claude Monet because of its responsiveness to sunlight. Images of the future (UFOs and spaceships) come first to the minds of many. But by far the most common themes in viewers' descriptions are medieval: a castle on the river, a knight in silver armor standing guard. Visitors often say of the building, "It makes me smile when I see it. It gives me energy."

Of course, some people are dubious about the nontraditional exterior of the Weisman, but even doubters admire the beautifully proportioned interior spaces, full of character yet perfectly suited to displaying art. The Julie and Babe Davis Gallery always features work from the museum's permanent collection; the rest of the galleries are divided between temporary exhibitions and art from the museum's collection. Since its opening the museum has displayed elegant Italian fifteenth-century drawings, thousand-year-old Native American Mimbres bowls, photographs of rock singer Bruce Springsteen, nineteenth-century Korean furniture, the Russian painter Kazimir Malevich's constructivist squares, and a great variety of work by American artists: giant Robert Motherwell abstract impressionist paintings, Marsden Hartley's abstractions of Maine landscapes, Georgia O'Keeffe's 1927 painting of poppies, Donald Judd's cool minimalist sculpture, and Edward and Nancy Kienholz's funky environmental installation, *Pedicord Apts*. Contemporary artists have suspended from the gallery ceilings everything from video monitors to thousands of roses.

Although the galleries have high ceilings (22 feet; 55 feet to the top of the tallest skylight well), they display diverse sizes and styles of art harmoniously. One tribute to the galleries Gehry designed is that more than one artist whose work has been shown at the Weisman has remarked that the galleries seemed to have been created just for his or her art – and the work of these artists was markedly different.

The windows of the Dolly Fiterman Riverview Gallery on the west side of the museum offer a constantly changing view of the Mississippi and downtown Minneapolis. This was intended to be the main hospitality space for the museum. Exhibit openings, dinners, weddings, bar mitzvahs, scholarly conferences, lectures, workshops for kids and families, senior proms, award ceremonies, and corporate holiday parties all take place here.

In an art study room honoring donors Malcolm and Louise McCannel, both freshmen art classes and academic scholars examine objects from the museum's collection, up close and personal. Students sprawl on the floors in the museum to draw the architecture and the art. The Hudson and Ione Walker Art Rental Gallery in the museum store makes available real works of art that students, faculty, and staff can live with in their offices and homes. The Weisman Family Seminar Room is a space for meetings, classes, and lectures. The William G. Shepherd auditorium, named for beloved former provost and museum mentor Jerry Shepherd, has heard many lectures and symposia – as well as diverse music. String quartets, experimental music groups, punk rock, reggae, and folk musicians give concerts here. Jokingly called "Jerry's Danceteria," the Shepherd Room is the site of the museum's annual Funk at the Fred student mixer during Welcome Week at the start of the school year. The purpose of the event is not to create new art history majors but to invite freshmen into the museum so they discover and experience it as a nonintimidating place that can be part of their regular routine at the university. It works!

A small balcony off the Riverview Gallery offers a lookout over the Mississippi, and a larger outdoor public terrace on the level above (which houses the museum's administrative offices) provides a spectacular panoramic view of the city, the university, and the river.

## THE ARCHITECT

Frank Gehry, best known for his city-transforming Guggenheim museum in Bilbao, Spain, was the unanimous choice of the museum's architect selection committee. He had previously designed warehouse renovations in Los Angeles as a space for contemporary art, but the Weisman was the first art museum he designed in its entirety. He is also known in Minneapolis and St. Paul as the creator of a huge glass-scaled fish in the Minneapolis Sculpture Garden. He won architecture's equivalent of the Nobel Prize, the Pritzker Prize, in 1989, and the American Institute of Architects' Gold Medal in 1999. He is very likely the most famous architect working today.

When Gehry first met with museum representatives at the university, he listened intently to their hopes and dreams. His early models were restrained; the building took on its unique character as the design progressed. Function never took a back seat to design in the discussions; the building was completed on time and on budget, but design did not finish in second place.

Most cities in the Midwest have exploited their urban rivers for industrial rather than scenic potential. The university agreed that the museum should connect with the Mississippi — one of the great rivers of the world — as much as with the campus. The most obvious way to do this might have been with a glass wall facing the river, but a major challenge was the Washington Avenue Bridge — a looming, unlovely neighbor. Gehry's solution was to "corrugate" the west side of the museum, the side that overlooks the river and the bridge. Trapezoids and other geometric window openings frame views up and down the river, offering not a panorama but a series of small snapshots that keep the river, not the bridge, in focus.

## THE MUSEUM

University of Minnesota president Lotus Coffman founded the Little Gallery in 1934. He believed in the power of art to transform lives and in its essential place at a great university. The first director of the museum was a young man from an artistic local family – Hudson Walker, grandson of Minneapolis's lumber magnate T. B. Walker, founder of the Walker Art Center. Walker championed the avant-garde artists of his day: Marsden Hartley, Arthur Dove, Alfred Maurer, Max Weber, and others who brought European modernism to this country. When Walker died in 1976, the collection of American art that he formed with his wife, Ione, came as a bequest to the museum.

The museum was named for businessman, art collector, and philanthropist Frederick Rand Weisman, who was born in Minneapolis in 1912 to Russian immigrant parents. He moved to Los Angeles with his mother when he was six but returned to visit his father in the summers. He studied at the University of Minnesota in the 1930s; though the cold weather and harsh economic climate quickly drove him back to California, he always considered the University of Minnesota his alma mater. Fred was a risk taker in business and in art collection, buying unknown artists as well as famous names.

The new museum building was funded entirely with private contributions from more than four hundred donors. The largest gift of $4 million came from the LaMothe family bequest; the smallest, $11.21, was collected by an art faculty member during a class. "There it stands like a silver knight, guarding the east bank [campus] from the MBAs," wrote a student the first year the museum was open. As this student recognized, Frank Gehry designed a museum for the University of Minnesota that boldly proclaims the essential value of art. Lotus Coffman would be proud.

**LYNDEL KING**
*DIRECTOR, WEISMAN ART MUSEUM*

# THE EXTERIOR CAN BE SEEN AS A TOUGH, GLEEFULLY MANIC WORK OF CUBIST SCULPTURE

**OR AS A GIANT BRUSHED STAINLESS-STEEL POPCORN KERNEL OR AS A WIZARD'S CASTLE IN SOME 23RD-CENTURY FAIRY TALE.**

*TIME*, JANUARY 3, 1994

Exit Only     Entrance

# GEHRY HAS DESIGNED AN INTERIOR SPACE OF BREATHTAKING SIMPLICITY THAT IS SIMULTANEOUSLY SERENE AND ANIMATED

*ARCHITECTURE MINNESOTA*, JANUARY/FEBRUARY 1994

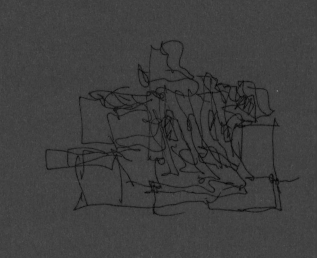

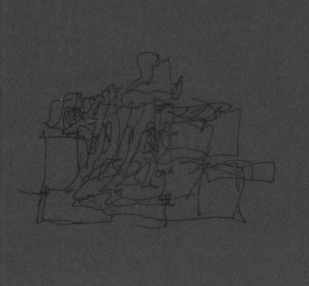

WRY HUMOR AND DYNAMIC LOOSENESS
PERMEATE THIS PROJECT – BUT NEVER AT
THE COST OF FUNCTION.

*THE OREGONIAN*, JANUARY 1, 1994

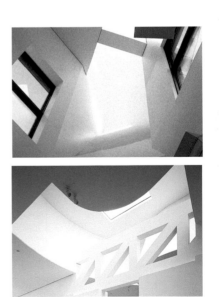

**A FABULOUS PLACE TO ENCOUNTER ART.**
**FROM THE MOMENT YOU ENTER ...**

## YOU GET THE IDEA THAT YOUR VISIT WILL NOT ONLY BE WORTHWHILE, BUT PROBABLY EVEN FUN.

*STAR TRIBUNE*, NOVEMBER 21, 1993

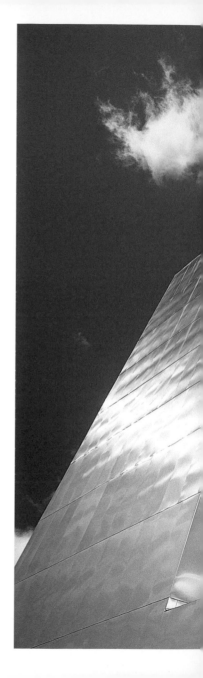

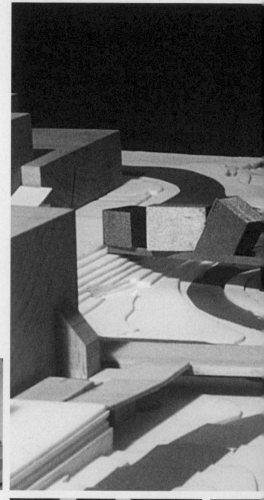

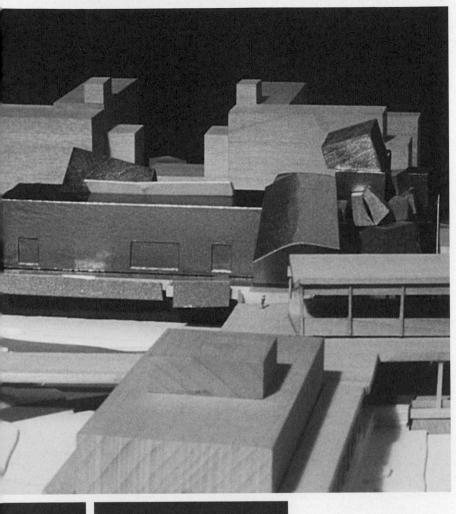

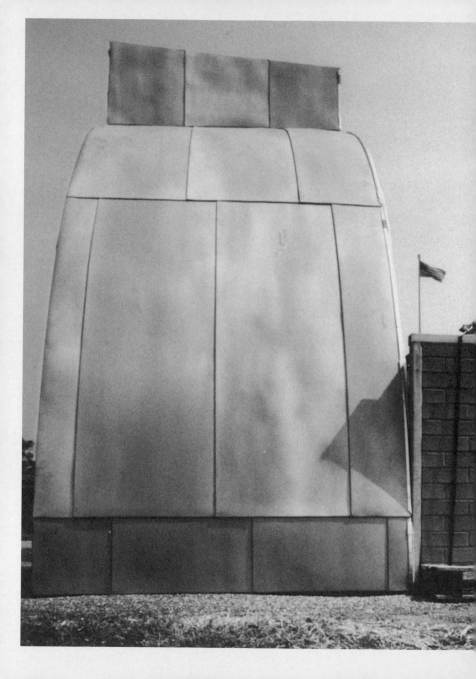

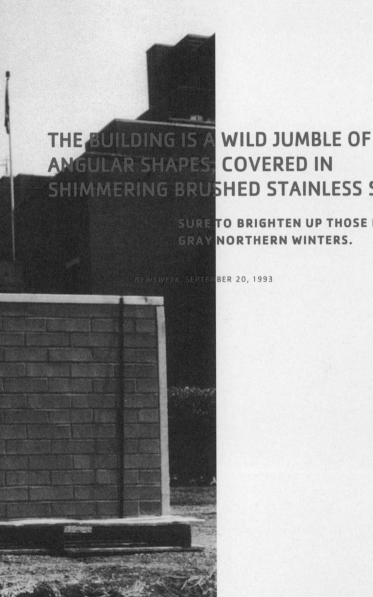

THE BUILDING IS A WILD JUMBLE OF
ANGULAR SHAPES, COVERED IN
SHIMMERING BRUSHED STAINLESS STEEL

SURE TO BRIGHTEN UP THOSE LONG,
GRAY NORTHERN WINTERS.

*NEWSWEEK, SEPTEMBER 20, 1993*

# THE GENIUS OF THIS PLACE IS THE IDEA THAT A UNIVERSITY ART MUSEUM SHOULDN'T BE DESIGNED TO KEEP THE LID ON EVERYTHING ART STANDS FOR.

**IT SHOULD DO EVERYTHING IT CAN TO TURN THE CONTENTS LOOSE.**

*NEW YORK TIMES*, DECEMBER 12, 1993

Published by Frederick R.
Weisman Art Museum
University of Minnesota
333 East River Road
Minneapolis, MN 55455
Phone: (612) 625-9494
www.weisman.umn.edu

Distributed by the University
of Minnesota Press
111 Third Avenue South
Suite 290
Minneapolis, MN 55401
www.upress.umn.edu

ISBN 0-8166-4504-3

A Cataloging-in-Publication
record for this book is
available from the Library
of Congress.

Book design by Gail Wiener
Cover photograph by
Bob Firth
Printed by Shapco Printing,
Inc., Minneapolis

**BUILDING CREDITS**

*Design Architects*
**Gehry Partners, LLP**

*Design Principal*
Frank O. Gehry, FAIA

*Managing Principals*
Robert Hale, Jr., AIA
Randy Jefferson, AIA

*Project Designer*
Edwin Chan

*Executive Architect*
**Meyer Scherer &
Rockcastle, Ltd.**

*Project Manager*
Jeffrey Scherer

*Project Architect*
John Cook

*Project Team Leader*
David Zenk

*Structural Engineers*
**Meyer, Borgman &
Johnson, Inc.**

*Civil Engineer*
**Progressive Consulting
Engineers**

*Mechanical/
Electrical Engineers*
**Ericksen, Ellison &
Associates**

*Lighting Consultants*
**PHA Lighting Design, Inc.**

*Landscape Architects*
**Damon Farber &
Associates, Inc.**

**PHOTO CREDITS**

*Paul Bichler* pages **19**
(insets), **60–61** (spread), **40**

*Chris Faust* pages **32**
(insets), **36** (inset), **37**
(inset), **38–39, 61** (insets)

*Bob Firth* pages **24** (top),
**25, 58–59, 62–63**

*Bob Fogt* page **34**

*Gehry Partners, LLP*
pages **10, 65, 66–67, 72–73,
78** (top), **79**

*Shawn Smith* pages **1,
2–3, 4–5, 12, 26, 36–37**
(spread), **54, 64**

*Weisman Art Museum*
pages **21** (bottom two
images), **24** (bottom), **46–47,
49** (top), **50–51, 52, 53, 68,
70–71, 73** (middle), **74–75,
76–77**

*Gail Wiener* pages **18–19**
(spread), **22–23**

*Don F. Wong* pages **16–17,
20, 21** (top and middle),
**30–31, 32–33** (spread), **35,
44–45, 48–49** (spread and
bottom image), **69** (inset), **78**
(bottom)